IT'S TIME TO EAT SHRIMP TEMPURA ROLL

It's Time to Eat SHRIMP TEMPURA ROLL

Walter the Educator

Silent King Books
A WhichHead Entertainment Imprint

Copyright © 2024 by Walter the Educator

All rights reserved. No part of this book may be reproduced in any manner whatsoever without written per- mission except in the case of brief quotations embodied in critical articles and reviews.

First Printing, 2024

Disclaimer

This book is a literary work; the story is not about specific persons, locations, situations, and/or circumstances unless mentioned in a historical context. Any resemblance to real persons, locations, situations, and/or circumstances is coincidental. This book is for entertainment and informational purposes only. The author and publisher offer this information without warranties expressed or implied. No matter the grounds, neither the author nor the publisher will be accountable for any losses, injuries, or other damages caused by the reader's use of this book. The use of this book acknowledges an understanding and acceptance of this disclaimer.

It's Time to Eat SHRIMP TEMPURA ROLL is a collectible early learning book by Walter the Educator suitable for all ages belonging to Walter the Educator's Time to Eat Book Series. Collect more books at WaltertheEducator.com

USE THE EXTRA SPACE TO TAKE NOTES AND DOCUMENT YOUR MEMORIES

SHRIMP TEMPURA ROLL

Shrimp tempura roll, crunchy and tight,

It's Time to Eat Shrimp Tempura Roll

Wrapped in rice and oh-so-white.

Inside the roll, a shrimp surprise,

Golden and crispy, the perfect size.

Dip it in sauce, give it a try,

Soy or sweet, oh my, oh my!

One little bite, and then one more,

Shrimp tempura's a tasty score.

The shrimp's cooked crisp, the rice is soft,

Each bite is chewy, never too tough.

Wrapped in seaweed, a green embrace,

It's sushi time, let's find our place!

Tiny white seeds, sprinkled on top,

Each little roll is a fun food stop.

With chopsticks or hands, take a bite,

Shrimp tempura roll feels just right.

It's Time to Eat
Shrimp Tempura Roll

The shrimp inside is crunchy and bright,

Hidden in rice, tucked in tight.

Bite into one, feel the crunch,

Shrimp tempura's great for lunch!

One for you and one for me,

A plate of rolls for us to see.

Shrimp tempura, fresh and neat,

A sushi snack that can't be beat.

From the sea to the chef's hand,

Shrimp tempura's made so grand.

Rolled with care, sliced with love,

It's a treat sent from above!

When you're hungry, it's the best,

A special roll, it's not like the rest.

Crispy, chewy, soft, and mild,

It's Time to Eat Shrimp Tempura Roll

Shrimp tempura makes you smile.

Add a slice of avocado, green and bright,

Or cucumber, crunchy and light.

Shrimp tempura roll's a tasty friend,

A yummy snack that never ends.

So grab a roll, take a seat,

Shrimp tempura's ready to eat.

A roll of joy, so tasty and fun,

It's Time to Eat Shrimp Tempura Roll

Shrimp tempura roll for everyone!

ABOUT THE CREATOR

Walter the Educator is one of the pseudonyms for Walter Anderson. Formally educated in Chemistry, Business, and Education, he is an educator, an author, a diverse entrepreneur, and he is the son of a disabled war veteran. "Walter the Educator" shares his time between educating and creating. He holds interests and owns several creative projects that entertain, enlighten, enhance, and educate, hoping to inspire and motivate you. Follow, find new works, and stay up to date with Walter the Educator™

at WaltertheEducator.com

Milton Keynes UK
Ingram Content Group UK Ltd.
UKHW022115251124
451529UK00012B/525